Enlightening Words and Wisdom

Birister Sharma

Dedicated to my loving wife....

Pallabi Devi Sharma

I surrendered to you, O my Lord......

"Om Namah Shivaya"

One Word

Your life is always in your hands. It is up to you what you want to do with your life. You are your own friend; you are your own foe.

If you do good deeds in your life, then you will become your own best friend. On the other hand, if you do bad deeds in your life, then you will become your own worst foe.

Everything depends upon your. You are the master of your own life.

Only you can rule your own life. Only you can change your own life.

If you can change your thoughts, you can change your mind. If you can change your mind, you can change your attitudes.

If you can change your attitudes, you can change your habits. If you can change your habits, you can change your life.

If you can change your life, you can change your world.

Nobody can transform you. Only you can transform yourself. You can transform yourself when you know your thoughts, when you know your mind, when you know your attitudes, when you know your habits, and when you know yourself.

~***~

1

Nobody can stop you to become amazing in your life, but it is up to you....

~***~

2

With an attitude of 'I Can DoAanything...' you can accomplish anything in your life...

~***~

3

It is only your positive mindset which will hold you tight in every harsh thunderstorm of your life....

~***~

4

Life is short and beautiful.... Don't forget to celebrate your life...

~***~

5

A prepared man never loses anything in his life....

~***~

6

Be always careful in your life.

Whatever you do in your life whether good or bad, everything reflects back to you.

~***~

7

If you want to succeed in your life, then attain your inner strength.

If you want to achieve something great in your life, then unearth your inner strength.

~***~

8

Encourage yourself no matter whatsoever happens in your life.

If you fail in every endeavor of your life, even never stop to encourage yourself.

Your encouragement is the ladder of your success.

~***~

9

You've infinite energy and power within you.

You just need to unearth it from deep inside you.

~***~

10

Your luck is disguised in the form of your hard works.

Your luck is much closer to you if you know how to make it yourself.

Your luck will find you itself.

~***~

11

Try to understand yourself and your time. And utilize it in your own way.

If you know how to use your time, you'll learn how to live your life.

Always try to become natural.

12

You've to take your own time. You never get anything in a hurry.

Even you're not grown up in a day or overnight.

Hurry brings you nothing but worry.

~***~

13

You've to change with time.

Always try to change yourself for good reasons.

But never try to change yourself for the wrong reasons.

Never get afraid to change yourself for good, because only your good change will bring a huge difference in this world.

~***~

14

Your habits are very powerful. The way you cultivate your habits the way you become.

Good habits make good life. And bad habits make bad life.

Never allow your habits to control you, but control your habits.

~***~

15

You're born with natural talents.

You've infinite potentials hidden within you.

You've to awaken your sleeping natural talents.

Awake your natural talents, and enjoy the beauties of this world.

∼***∽

16

If you want to survive in this world, then you've to change yourself according to time, place and need.

∼***∽

17

Your past is already gone forever.

Your past has no use in your present moment.

~***~

18

Live your life now.

Live your life today.

Live your life in present.

Your past is already gone.

Your present is on.

Forget it like a nightmare.

Forget it forever.

Your present is a new dawn.

It brings you new hope and bliss.

~***~

19

Accept who you're.

Accept what you're.

Accept what you are doing right now.

Accept where you are right now.

Accept what you have actually in your life.

~***~

20

Learn to enjoy your life.

Learn to enjoy your world.

Life is too short.

Nothing is permanent.

Both success and failure.

Both happiness and sorrows.

Like day and night.

Enjoy your success.

Enjoy your failure.

Enjoy your happiness.

Enjoy your sorrows.

Accept the realities of life.

But never regret.

Stop expecting too much.

Set your goal and go for it.

You will get what you're made for.

~***~

21

If you're successful in your life, then you're only responsible for your success.

If you fail in your life, then you're only responsible for your failure.

You will never share your success or failure with anybody in your life.

~***~

22

You're like the goldsmith of your life.

You can convert your life in any form or any design of jewels.

~***~

23

It is always up to you what you want in your life: success or failure; happiness or unhappiness.

~***~

24

Nobody will become a better cook than you in your life,

Because you know what are the best ingredients for your life.

~***~

You're responsible for yourself, whatever you think;

Whatever you plan; whatever you decide; whatever you prepare; and whatever you act.

Your life is like a white paper.

Whether you write something about it,

Or you leave it blank.

Or you tear it.

Whether you write success on it,

Or you write failure on it.

Everything depends upon you.

You've to think yourself.

You've to plan yourself.

You've to decide yourself.

You've to prepare yourself.

You've to act yourself.

After all, you're the sole responsible for your own life.

~***~

26

You can only develop yourself when you know your hidden treasures of skills and talents.

~***~

27

Everything is within you.

You've a tremendous treasure house lying within you.

You can do anything in your life.

Nothing is impossible for you.

You can achieve any success in your life.

You can touch any summit in your life.

Nobody can stop you.

But you've to know your hidden potentials.

You've to reinvent yourself.

Once you'll know your hidden skills and talents, then nobody will ever dare to stop you to reach your goal.

You'll become the master of your destiny.

You'll become the sole maker of your fortune.

Reinvent yourself.

Reinvent your life.

Reinvent your world.

∼***∼

28

Action is your life.

Without action your life is impossible.

It is only your action which makes your life possible.

Your action gives you new movements in your life.

Your action gives you new ways in your life.

Your action gives you new purpose in your world.

∼***∼

With your action you're alive. Without action, you'll die.

A man becomes a complete man with his action.

~***~

Action means your life.

Inaction means your death.

You can't live without action.

You've to act in order to live your life.

Your action is the only source of your happiness.

Your action is the only source of your progress.

Your action is the only source of your success.

Your action is the only source of your peace.

No action, there is no happiness.

No action, there is no progress.

No action, there is no success.

No action, there is no peace.

It is only your action which gives you the meaning of your life.

It is only your action which shows you the purpose of your life.

You're born to act.

But not to remain idle.

Your action brings you happiness and prosperities in your life.

But your inaction brings you unhappiness and adversities in your life.

Every living creature on this earth does some action in order to exist.

You're existed in this world because you're doing some action in your life.

Your persistence never pushes you into the door of downfall,

But it'll always hold you firmly,

It'll always lead you to the door of rising great success.

Persistence is the natural order.

It is the fundamental law of our life.

Without it, nobody could live in this world.

All the living creatures on this earth are bound or abided by persistence.

Nobody could deny it or alter it.

We all are bound and abided to work with persistence to live in this world.

Persistence is the only key to unlock your ceased fortune.

With persistence, you could achieve anything in your life.

~***~

Focus makes you trained and disciplined in your life, and give you the right direction.

Focus your mind, body and soul only on your chosen goal.

Forget the other insignificant things in your life.

Go for it!

Nobody will ever dare to obstruct you on the path of your success.

~***~

32

33

Your focus is one of the key factors of your grand success.

Your focus opens your closed mind.

Your focus awakes your dizzy heart.

Your focus salvages your soul.

Your focus gives you new directions in your life.

Your focus enlightens your dark world.

If you want grand success in your life,

Then focus on your chosen goal.

Never divert your mind, heart and soul.

Only focus on your aims and objectives.

You'll always witness your bright success and glory.

Only focus on your goals.

Only focus on your life.

Only focus on your world.

Your success is always decided by your focus.

~***~

34

Enjoy your failure like you enjoy your success.

Welcome it with your open mind and heart.

Treat it as your teacher.

Learn from it.

Improve yourself.

But, never allow it to rule you.

Tame it as your galloping horse.

And march ahead towards the road to your success.

~***~

35

Failure is only a momentary,

It's a temporary.

No doubt, it bends your road,

But it can't block your road.

Even success is not permanent,

You need your temperament.

Your hope is your golden ray,

Show you your hidden way.

Don't cry,

Never say die.

Believe yourself,

Work yourself.

Try to get up!

Try to rise up!

Don't make your heart weak,

Make your heart strong.

When you turn your failure into success,

Then you'll definitely get your sparkling success.

Never mind failure,

Your failure is the stepping-stone,

Which leads you to the ultimate milestone.

~***~

36

If you want wonders in your life,

Then always think positive and act positive.

If you want miracles in your life,

Then always think positive and act positive.

If you want everlasting happiness and peace in your life,

Then always think positive and act positive.

If you want to become a winner in your life,

Then always think positive and act positive.

If you want a grand success in your life,

Then always think positive and act positive.

~***~

37

If you want a good life,

Then always be positive whatever happens in your life.

If you want a happy life,

Then always be positive whatever happens in your life.

If you want a peaceful life,

Then always be positive whatever happens in your life.

If you want a successful life,

Then always be positive whatever happens in your life.

If you want a dignified life,

Then always be positive whatever happens in your life.

If you want a glorious life,

Then always be positive whatever happens in your life.

~***~

38

Your abilities are the ingredients and catalysts of your success.

Your abilities are your boon.

23

Always believe it.

No matter whatsoever happens in your life.

If you've abilities, then you've nothing to worry.

Your abilities will lead you towards your goal.

~***~

39

Believe in your abilities.

It can move away every Himalayan like task.

Believe in your abilities.

It is the only key to unlock your sealed door of success.

You're born with tremendous natural abilities.

Search it within you.

Nourish it every day.

Exploit it every moment.

Your abilities are your energy and power.

It is only your abilities which will make everything possible.

Always believe in your abilities.

~***~

40

You can only solve your problems of life by helping yourself.

But you can't solve your problems of life if you're running away from it.

～***～

41

The moment you stop helping yourself, you'll lose your own credentials of your life.

And the moment you start helping yourself, you'll regain your own credentials of your life.

Nobody will help you when you'll tumble down into the deep ditch.

It is only you who can scale yourself up.

Never wait for anybody.

Make yourself your own helping hand.

Only you can help yourself best.

Even Almighty God helps those who help themselves.

Help yourself.

Believe yourself.

Self-help is the best help.

~***~

42

Take your every small step

One by one

Step by step

Every day and every night

But never afraid of your small steps.

Your every small step will make a huge difference in your life.

Just keep continue your small steps.

Never forget that you too grow every day and every night

Slowly and slowly.

Step by step.

Nothing will grow or develop overnight.

It is the law of nature.

Your every small step will count in your growth and development.

Your success is not in taking big steps,

But converting your every small step into a big result.

~***~

43

An optimistic person sees possibility in every calamity. But a pessimistic person sees impossible in every golden opportunity.

~***~

44

Always decide to be happy in your life, no matter whatsoever happens in your life.

If you decide to be happy, then nobody can make you unhappy without your consent.

You are the maker of your own happiness.

~***~

45

*The best things will only happen in your life when you
expect the best things.*

∼***∼

46

Always expect the best, and always achieve the best.

*The way you expect, the way you think, the way you act,
and the way you become in your life.*

*The best product of your life is only produced by your best
expectation.*

∼***∼

47

Trust yourself before you trust anybody in your life.

Trusting yourself means you trust this universe.

With your trust, you can create your own universe.

~***~

48

Always see the silver lining in every tough situation in your life.

It gives you strength, energy and power to tackle every tough situation.

~***~

49

Celebrate your life every day.

Celebrate your life with every little thing.

Every little celebration makes you happy and brings happiness, prosperity and peace in your life.

~***~

50

Always take a positive view in your life; you will always see possibility in everything.

You will never divert in your life.

You will always find the right direction in every puzzling situation of your life.

~***~

51

Don't forget to have some fun in your life.

Don't make your life dull and lifeless.

You will never live your life in lifeless ambience.

Make your life like spring season even in the midst of autumn season of your life.

~***~

52

Every day is important in your life. Every day is a golden day for you.

Once you miss your golden day, you will miss it forever…

Don't misuse it.

Do something great and special thing in your life.

Always remember that every day counts in your life.

∼***∽

53

*Encourage yourself day and night until you will not receive
the sparkling energy and power of your courage and high spirit.*

*If you don't find encouragement from anyone in your life,
then encourage yourself….*

∼***∽

54

*Appreciate yourself whenever you do anything good in
your life.*

Don't expect any appreciation from anybody.

Appreciate yourself.

Nobody can appreciate you better than you yourself.

~***~

55

Your curiosity is the mother of your wisdom and knowledge.

Always keep alive your curiosity in your life.

~***~

56

Your perseverance is priceless.

There is no measure of your perseverance.

Nothing is impossible for you if you persevere in your life.

Your perseverance is the key to your success.

You can only build your life with your perseverance.

Never afraid of perseverance.

Your perseverance never kills you.

But, it makes you strong and powerful.

Only your idleness and procrastination will kill you.

Be always aware from these bitter enemies of your success.

Your perseverance always pays you grand price.

~***~

57

Focus on your present.

It is the golden moment to initiate something great in your life.

Never waste it.

Focus on your work.

Focus on your hard works and dedications.

Utilize your present moment in the constructive way.

Your future is always decided by the works you will execute in your present.

~***~

58

Focus! Focus! Focus!

Only focus on your present moment!

Your focus on your present moment is the only path to your greatest happiness, success, prosperity and peace.

~***~

59

If you imagine great, you will become great.

If you imagine the grand success, you will attain your grand success.

Your imagination is the replica of your reality.

Therefore, be careful before you imagine anything.

Because the way you imagine yourself, the way you will become in your actual life.

~***~

60

*Your imagination is the most powerful tool in your life,
because with the power of your imagination you can do anything
in your life. A sculptor before he carves any sculpture, he
imagines the image of the sculpture in his mind.*

~***~

61

Never scare of your mistakes.

Your mistakes are your great teachers.

It will teach you many greatest lessons about your life.

You will never learn anything if you never make mistakes.

Your mistakes will make you strong.

*Your mistakes will help you to uncluttered your latent
mind.*

Your mistakes will open the new door of opportunities.

Only with your mistakes, you can discover new things.

*There is nobody in this world that has never made any
mistakes.*

Learn from your mistakes.

But, never repeat the same mistakes.

Correct it straight away before you proceed further.

Mistakes are your best friends if you know how to gain wisdom and knowledge from it.

~***~

62

Never afraid of your mistakes. A man who never commits any mistake, he will never learn anything in his life. Your mistakes will make you mature and experienced.

Your mistakes will give you another opportunity to improve yourself.

~***~

63

Live in your present moment.

Focus on your present moment.

Never waste it.

Utilize it.

Think in your present moment.

Plan in your present moment.

Decide in your present moment.

Work in your present moment.

Enjoy in your present moment.

Make it special for you.

Make it successful for you.

Your life is always decided by your present moment.

Everything is in the hands of your present moment.

Live your life in your present moment.

Never leave anything for tomorrow.

Your present moment is your life.

Your present moment is your world.

You can do anything in your present moment.

~***~

64

What you can do in your present moment, you can't do anything once, it will slip away from your hands.

Your present moment is your life. Your past is your graveyard which is already buried. And your future is not yet born; it is in the womb of your present moment.

You have nothing to worry. Just concentrate on your present moment.

37

Your grand success is always waiting for you.

~***~

65

Create your own value.

Your life is the most valuable thing in this world.

You will become the way you give value to yourself.

Love yourself.

Care yourself.

Make yourself like a precious jewel.

You are the maker of your own life and world.

Give value to yourself.

Give value to everybody.

You are the first person to value yourself.

Nobody will value you if you can't value yourself.

~***~

66

There is nothing more valuable than your life. Love your life. Care your life. Enrich your life. Grow your life. Develop your life.

Make your life meaningful and purposeful. Live your life fully.

Make your life a complete package of love, happiness, success, prosperity and peace.

~*****~

67

Life is always depends on give and take.

The way you give, the way you will get.

You will never receive anything while giving nothing.

It is like no pain, no gain.

~*****~

68

Never expect different results in your life.

You will get what you give.

You will get what is deserved for you.

If you deliver good works, you will get good results.

This is the real philosophy of life.

Give and take.

No work, no result.

No pain, no gain.

You will only get one result at one time.

You will never get different results from one piece of work.

~***~

69

The seeds of good always germinate good plants. The seeds of bad always germinate bad plants.

You never expect good fruits from bad seeds.

You'll receive the way you give in your life.

You'll never expect different results from one piece of work

This is the law of life.

~***~

70

Never hesitate to gain experience in your life.

Your experience is the source of great knowledge.

Your experience never goes to waste.

Your experience will help you to live your life fully.

Your experience is your greatest teacher.

Your experience is your great guide.

Your experience is your pathfinder.

Only your experience will solve your problems.

Your experience makes you fearless.

Your experience will lead you to your great success.

~***~

71

Your experience is the biggest teacher in your life.

Like a teacher teaches you about the lessons which are in the textbook, in the same way your experience will teach you about the great lessons of life.

~***~

72

Never play the game of your life if you don't know its rules.

Learn the rules of your life.

Be the master of your life's rule.

You'll win any battle.

No Himalayan task will ever halt you from the path of your success.

Nobody will dare to defeat you.

You'll become an unbeatable warrior in your life.

You'll become like the king of this world.

~***~

73

If you suppose that your life is a game, then you've to learn its every rule in order to play your game and break its rules, and you would make your own rules later on.

~***~

74

Love is one of the most beautiful things in the entire universe. Love is the mother of everything. Its language is understood by every living creature of this world.

~***~

75

You're born to win.

You're born to become strong.

You're born to achieve something great.

You're born to become successful.

You're born to be a winner.

~***~

76

Aim High,

You've to touch the sky.

Aim high,

You've to reach the highest summit.

Aim High,

You've to shine like the star.

~***~

77

Always see big dreams,

See it with your open eyes,

Feel it with full consciousness,

Always think about it,

Always imagine it,

Always live with it,

Always keep it alive.

Always work for it.

One day, you'll realize your dream into reality.

~***~

78

Hard work guaranteed you success,

Hard work guaranteed you victory,

Hard work guaranteed you happiness,

Hard work guaranteed you prosperities.

~***~

79

Keep your rays of hope alive.

Your hopes give you new ways.

Your hopes give you new dawn.

Your hopes give you a new smile.

Your hopes give you new life.

Your hopes give you new strength.

Your hopes give you new destination.

Keep your rays of hope alive.

~***~

80

The taste of patience is the sweetest in the world. You've to wait again and again if you want to taste it.

~***~

81

With strong willpower,

The lame can walk.

With strong willpower,

The dumb can talk.

With strong willpower,

The deaf can hear.

With strong willpower,

The impossible becomes possible.

~***~

82

There is a great impact of both positive things and negative things in your life.

~***~

83

A brave man is a king.

He is like the lion.

He is like the giant mountain.

He is like the hard rock.

He is always ready to face any challenge.

He never accepts any defeat.

~***~

84

In your tough time, you've to become a source of encouragement of yourself.

~***~

85

Discover your natural skills and talents, and polish it, and see the great difference in your life.

~***~

86

Delete the word 'Fear' from your dictionary.

Defeat your fear with your self-believe, self-confidence, self-discipline and self-reliance.

Don't be the victim of fear.

Kill it before it will kill you.

Your fears are nothing but a self-created ghost.

Only you can drive away your fear.

~***~

87

Your brain is the creator of your great thoughts, great ideas, great plans and great decisions.

~***~

88

The real treasure is always within you.

Only you can discover it.

The real wealth is always within you.

Only you can discover it.

The real diamond is always within you.

Only you can discover it.

~***~

Before you make any choice in your life,

Think yourself.

Before you make any choice in your life,

Judge yourself.

Before you make any choice in your life,

Plan yourself.

Before you make any choice in your life,

Prepare yourself.

Good choices make you good.

Great choices make you great.

Bad choices make you bad.

You'll make your life the way you make choices in your life.

You'll be known by the choices you make in your life.

90

Obstacles never make you weak,

But, it'll make you stronger.

Obstacles never make you poor,

But, it'll make you rich.

Obstacles never make you a failure,

But, it'll make you successful.

Obstacles never make you a coward,

But, it'll make you brave.

Obstacles never make you an ordinary man,

But, it'll make you an extra-ordinary man.

~***~

91

Think big thing, you'll achieve a big thing.

Think small thing, you'll achieve small thing.

The way you think, the way you achieve.

The way you think, the way you become.

Be aware of your thinking!

Thinking makes you what you want to do in your life.

Thinking makes you what you want to become in your life.

Your thinking is the outline of your reality.

Think cautiously.

Think analytically.

Everything depends on your thinking.

Think today!

Act today!

~***~

92

Everything is possible if you plan well before you execute.

Take your time.

Think deeply.

Analyze thoroughly.

Plan well.

Then act well.

You'll definitely achieve whatever you want in your life.

Only proper planning will secure your life.

Nobody can do anything without making proper planning.

Your planning is the winning mantra of your life.

Plan today and make your life secure and successful.

~***~

93

If you see big dream, you'll achieve your big dream.

If you see small dream, you'll achieve small dream.

As you see your dream as you achieve in your reality.

Your dream is very powerful.

Believe in your dream.

~***~

94

Love your work.

Live with your work.

Work now, work today!

Never leave your work for tomorrow.

You'll never regain your lost work tomorrow.

Today is the best time to accomplish your work.

Your work cherishes your life and your world.

If you work today, you'll never sleep with an empty belly in your life.

If you work today, you'll able to fulfill all the basic needs of your life.

Your work is the source of everything.

Your work makes your life like heaven.

Work today! Live today!

~***~

95

Your smile is like a blooming flower.

Sweet and fragrant.

It adorns your life and your world.

Your smile is like a sparkling jewel.

Cute and beautiful.

It is the beauty of your life.

It is the magic of your world.

It is precious and priceless.

It is a source of your joy and happiness.

Wear it wherever you go and wherever you live.

Never allow it to fade away from your life.

Keep it alive in your life.

Keep it in your heart and soul.

Your smile is the most valuable asset of your life.

Always fill your life and your world with the sweetness of your smile.

Smile today. Live today.

~***~

96

Your life is how short or how prolonged.

Nobody can predict it.

You've only twenty-four hours in your hands.

You've to use a few seconds for yourself.

You've to manage a few minutes for yourself.

You've to spend a few hours for yourself.

Today's time is yours.

The sand of time never waits for you.

Once it'll slip away from you,

You'll never regain it tomorrow.

Today is your golden day.

Enjoy your life.

Enjoy in your world.

You've every right to enjoy your life fully!

~***~

97

Set your goal right from today.

Set your goal right now.

Your goal leads you in your life.

Your goal gives you new ways in your life.

Your goal gives you new directions in your life.

Without goals, you can't move ahead in your life.

Without goals, you can't achieve anything in your life.

If you've a goal, then nobody can stop you.

You'll find your vision and mission of life.

You'll discover your hidden potentials.

You'll become unstoppable.

You'll reach wherever you want in your life.

You'll touch the summit of every great success and glory.

Never forget to set your goal.

Set your goal right from today.

Set your goal right now.

~***~

98

Never try to escape from the problems of your life like a coward.

Face your every problem with bold hearts.

~***~

99

You're the mirror of yourself.

You'll always see your own reflections.

You'll never hide yourself.

~***~

100

You can't change everybody in this world.

Only you can change yourself.

If you know how to change yourself, you'll know how to change your own life.

If you know how to change your own life, you'll know how to change your own world.

If you know how to change your own world, you'll know how to change this world.

~***~

101

If the bad things are happening in your life at the moment, it means your good things are yet to come.

~***~

About the author:

Birister Sharma is a full time author. He is also an avid reader. He loves reading, writing, and motivation. He has penned down dozens of self-help motivational books and novels so far.

You may contact him @ <u>birister2007@gmail.com</u>

* 9 7 9 8 8 8 9 2 3 7 4 5 7 *